SELF-LOVE Affirmation Journal

Developed by: Athena Salisbury, CEO of Goddess Adorn

goddessadorn.com

empoweredlivinginc.net

Adorn-Me begins with...

Adorn: verb: To enhance the appearance of especially with beautiful objects
-Websters dictionary

Beginning the journey to self-love is hard.
Finding the strength to love you can be a struggle at times. Learning how to love you and be ok with your uniqueness is key.
You have one life.
You must find the joy within you daily.
Forget yesterday.
Renew the love of you now.
Enjoy your journey to self-love.

Athena Salisbury - Goddess Adorn

Love jewelry, find me on all social media platforms @goddessadornme

I'm able to love me more because...

I am able to allow myself grace because...

Things I will achieve are...

_____
_____
_____
_____
_____
_____
_____
_____
_____
_____
_____
_____
_____
_____
_____
_____
_____
_____
_____
_____
_____
_____
_____
_____
_____
_____

"Believing in yourself is half the battle"

Things I will achieve are...

Things I will achieve are...

"Believing in yourself is half the battle"

Things I will achieve are...

Things I will achieve are...

_____
_____
_____
_____
_____
_____
_____
_____
_____
_____
_____
_____
_____
_____
_____
_____
_____
_____
_____
_____
_____
_____
_____

"Believing in yourself is half the battle"

Things I will achieve are...

Things I will achieve are...

_____
_____
_____
_____
_____
_____
_____
_____
_____
_____
_____
_____
_____
_____
_____
_____
_____
_____
_____
_____
_____
_____
_____
_____

"Believing in yourself is half the battle"

Write it down

Positive Affirmation

Date: _____

Today I want to feel...

_____
_____
_____
_____

Today I will show myself grace by...

_____
_____
_____
_____

A new way I will embrace all of me today is...

_____
_____
_____
_____

POUR LOVE INTO YOURSELF

Positive Affirmation

Date: _____

Today I want to feel...

_____
_____
_____
_____

Today I will show myself grace by...

_____
_____
_____
_____

A new way I will embrace all of me today is...

_____
_____
_____
_____

POUR LOVE INTO YOURSELF

Positive Affirmation

Date: _____

Today I want to feel...

_____
_____
_____
_____

Today I will show myself grace by...

_____
_____
_____
_____

A new way I will embrace all of me today is...

_____
_____
_____
_____

POUR LOVE INTO YOURSELF

Positive Affirmation

Date: _____

Today I want to feel...

_____
_____
_____
_____

Today I will show myself grace by...

_____
_____
_____
_____

A new way I will embrace all of me today is...

_____
_____
_____
_____

POUR LOVE INTO YOURSELF

Positive Affirmation

Date: _____

Today I want to feel...

_____
_____
_____
_____

Today I will show myself grace by...

_____
_____
_____
_____

A new way I will embrace all of me today is...

_____
_____
_____
_____

POUR LOVE INTO YOURSELF

Positive Affirmation

Date: _____

Today I want to feel...

Today I will show myself grace by...

A new way I will embrace all of me today is...

POUR LOVE INTO YOURSELF

Positive Affirmation

Date: _____

Today I want to feel...

_____
_____
_____
_____

Today I will show myself grace by...

_____
_____
_____
_____

A new way I will embrace all of me today is...

_____
_____
_____
_____

POUR LOVE INTO YOURSELF

Positive Affirmation

Date: _____

Today I want to feel...

_____
_____
_____
_____

Today I will show myself grace by...

_____
_____
_____
_____

A new way I will embrace all of me today is...

_____
_____
_____
_____

POUR LOVE INTO YOURSELF

Positive Affirmation

Date: _____

Today I want to feel...

_____
_____
_____
_____

Today I will show myself grace by...

_____
_____
_____
_____

A new way I will embrace all of me today is...

_____
_____
_____
_____

POUR LOVE INTO YOURSELF

Positive Affirmation

Date: _____

Today I want to feel...

_____
_____
_____
_____

Today I will show myself grace by...

_____
_____
_____
_____

A new way I will embrace all of me today is...

_____
_____
_____
_____

POUR LOVE INTO YOURSELF

Positive Affirmation

Date: _____

Today I want to feel...

_____
_____
_____
_____

Today I will show myself grace by...

_____
_____
_____
_____

A new way I will embrace all of me today is...

_____
_____
_____
_____

POUR LOVE INTO YOURSELF

Positive Affirmation

Date: _____

Today I want to feel...

_____
_____
_____
_____

Today I will show myself grace by...

_____
_____
_____
_____

A new way I will embrace all of me today is...

_____
_____
_____
_____

POUR LOVE INTO YOURSELF

Positive Affirmation

Date: _____

Today I want to feel...

_____
_____
_____
_____

Today I will show myself grace by...

_____
_____
_____
_____

A new way I will embrace all of me today is...

_____
_____
_____
_____

Pour love into yourself

Positive Affirmation

Date: _____

Today I want to feel...

_____
_____
_____
_____

Today I will show myself grace by...

_____
_____
_____
_____

A new way I will embrace all of me today is...

_____
_____
_____
_____

POUR LOVE INTO YOURSELF

Positive Affirmation

Date: _____

Today I want to feel...

_____
_____
_____
_____

Today I will show myself grace by...

_____
_____
_____
_____

A new way I will embrace all of me today is...

_____
_____
_____
_____

POUR LOVE INTO YOURSELF

Positive Affirmation

Date: _____

Today I want to feel...

_____
_____
_____
_____

Today I will show myself grace by...

_____
_____
_____
_____

A new way I will embrace all of me today is...

_____
_____
_____
_____

POUR LOVE INTO YOURSELF

Positive Affirmation

Date: _____

Today I want to feel...

_____
_____
_____

Today I will show myself grace by...

_____
_____
_____

A new way I will embrace all of me today is...

_____
_____
_____

POUR LOVE INTO YOURSELF

Positive Affirmation

Date: _____

Today I want to feel...

_____
_____
_____
_____

Today I will show myself grace by...

_____
_____
_____
_____

A new way I will embrace all of me today is...

_____
_____
_____
_____

POUR LOVE INTO YOURSELF

Positive Affirmation

Date: _____

Today I want to feel...

_____
_____
_____
_____

Today I will show myself grace by...

_____
_____
_____
_____

A new way I will embrace all of me today is...

_____
_____
_____
_____

POUR LOVE INTO YOURSELF

Positive Affirmation

Date: _____

Today I want to feel...

_____
_____
_____
_____

Today I will show myself grace by...

_____
_____
_____
_____

A new way I will embrace all of me today is...

_____
_____
_____
_____

POUR LOVE INTO YOURSELF

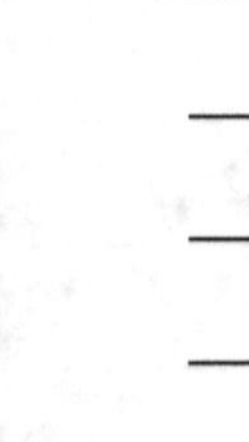

Self-Expression

Leave it here. Take it a step further & burn the page to release it

Writing is self-healing

3 minute journaling

3 minute journaling

3 minute journaling

3 minute journaling

3 minute journaling

3 minute journaling

How are you?

How are you?

How are you?

How are you?

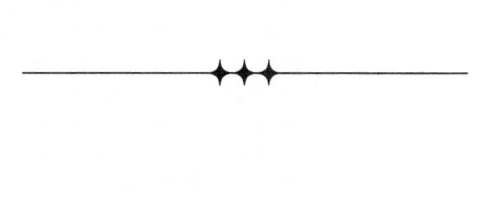

Write a letter to yourself. What do you love about you? How do you embrace all of you? Do this periodically

"Adorn yourself so others know your worth"

Athena Salisbury - Goddess Adorn

Free your thoughts

Release and Leave it here

Freestyle Journaling

Freestyle Journaling

Freestyle
Journaling

Freestyle Journaling

Freestyle Journaling

Freestyle Journaling

Freestyle
Journaling

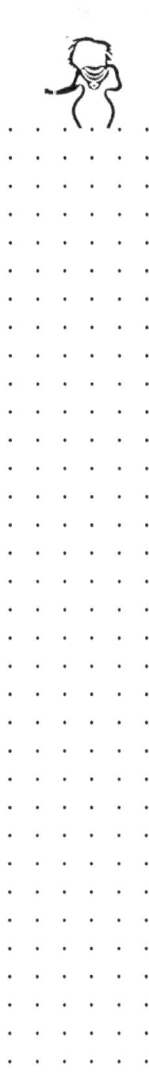

www.ingramcontent.com/pod-product-compliance
Lightning Source LLC
Chambersburg PA
CBHW072052110526
44590CB00018B/3135